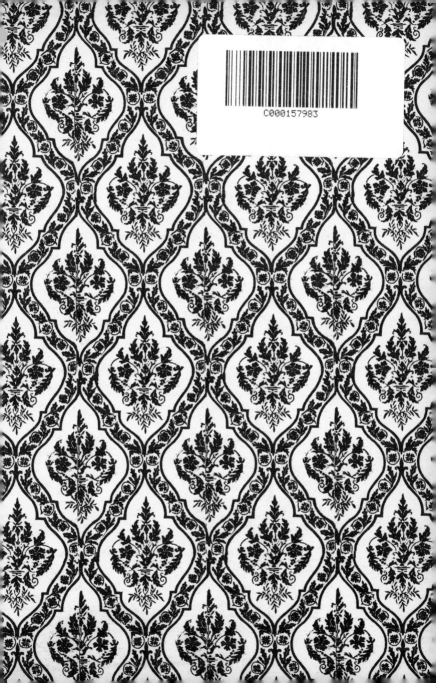

THE
NIGHTMARE
OF A VICTORIAN BESTSELLER

First published in 2002 by
Short Books
15 Highbury Terrace
London N5 1UP

10 9 8 7 6 5 4 3 2 1

A CIP catalogue record for this book
is available from the British Library.

ISBN 1-904095-17-8

Printed in Great Britain by
Bookmarque Ltd, Croydon, Surrey

THE NIGHTMARE

OF A VICTORIAN BESTSELLER

Martin Tupper's 'Proverbial Philosophy'

BRIAN THOMPSON

✳ SHORT BOOKS

FOR ARABELLA

Martin Tupper aged 40

One smoky summer's evening in the 1860s, when time lay heavy in North London, the daughters of Karl Marx teased him into playing a popular schoolroom paper game. He was given a series of written questions about his likes and dislikes which he had to answer as truthfully as possible. As he went along there were few surprises and some sly jokes. Marx's favourite virtue in men was strength; in women, weakness. His favourite colour was red. The vice he most excused in other people – and this may have been more of the truth than he intended – was gullibility. He came at last to answer the question 'Your aversion'? Unhesitatingly his pen slashed out a name that caused squeals of delighted laughter.

Marx's pet aversion proved to his girls that Pappi could be just as skittish and absurd as the next man. Everyone knew of the ridiculous Martin Tupper,

Esq., whose one great literary work could be found decorating the shelves of bourgeois sitting-rooms all over London, indeed throughout the British Isles. Many a young couple had been given the book on their wedding day and many an old man reached for his Tupper in times of woe. In the cruel light cast by the tricky, argumentative, fearsomely intelligent Marx household, to make Martin Tupper your aversion instead of mouse droppings or hymn-singing, spinach or brass-band concerts was the perfect response.

The two men had never met. To the Marx family, Tupper was hardly human at all. He was a condition, like flu in winter or what Londoners described as 'summer fever', a mild form of dysentery that sprang (as they thought) from the choked and heated drains. He was one of those minor irritations of Victorian England that, come the glorious day, would be swept away into the dustbin of history. Though it is very unlikely Marx had ever read any of Tupper's works, the mere name was like a paper target pinned to the breast of a condemned man. There was a fine irony here. Tupper's crime was being popular. Nobody except a few friends and enemies had ever heard of Karl Marx.

In 1830, Oxford was a university wakening from the intellectual torpor that had engrossed it in the 18th century. The University Debating Society was five years old and met in rooms behind Wyatt's on The High. Iron garden benches were laid out to replicate in miniature the Chamber of the House of Commons. A nervy and unsmiling young man called Gladstone was that year's President. At Westminster, the question of parliamentary reform was in the air, which gave the infant that became the Oxford Union its clamour and urgency. There were many intelligent men – and Gladstone was one of them – who thought they saw in Reform the beginning of the end of all civilisation, all Englishness as it was previously understood.

There was by now, however, no question but that it would come. In June 1830 the violently reactionary George IV died and was succeeded by that amiable and bluff old cove, William IV, who saw no great harm in extending the franchise. The King was given to walking about the streets of London, tipping his hat to anyone he met. What gave the Reform issue its impetus were events later that summer, when all Europe was engulfed in revolutionary political turmoil. Principles suddenly gave way to prudence. The young gentlemen of the University Debating Society had, by the end of 1830, been forced to accept that for the most part their lives would be led in contradiction to their fathers' most cherished beliefs.

Perhaps most vexing of all to a conservative cast of mind was the emergence of that new phemonenon, public opinion. What it was, and how it would act upon events in the future, no one could be sure. However, those who had never before had a voice and now found one in the flourishing radical press had already pointed out some uncomfortable truths. Lancashire was four times as populous as Cornwall, for example, and was taxed at six or seven times the rate. Unfortunately for advocates of leaving things as they were, Cornwall returned three times as many MPs. One did not need to be a revolutionary firebrand to see that this was not a situation likely to endure for very much longer.

There were still quite as many outrageous idlers and coxcombs in the university as there always had been – riding to hounds, running up debts against their tailor or bootmaker, breaking window glass and yahooing into the small hours. The dons, as any college waiter could attest, kept up enough eccentricity to make them a delight to their students and a scandal to foreigners. But not at Christ Church. Ruskin, who went up in 1836, remembered morning service there in this way:

> Every man in his place, according to his rank, age and learning; every man of sense or heart there recognising that he was either fulfilling, or being prepared to fill, the gravest duties required of Englishmen.

In 1830, the Reverend Mr Biscoe's course in Aristotle at Christ Church was already an instance of this earnestness. Each week his class assembled, among others, two future Governors-General of India; a Governor-General of Canada; Lord Lincoln, the eldest son of the Duke of Newcastle, and his friend from Eton days, W. E. Gladstone. Three future Bishops and a Chancellor of the Exchequer jostled for seats.

Also present was Mr Martin Farquhar Tupper, a short, plump and lovably innocent young man who was distinguished from his companions by two things. He was already engaged to be married and he spoke with such a profound stutter that Mr Biscoe despaired of him ever passing the viva required for graduation. 'There, there, Mr Tupper,' he would say soothingly, 'I am sure you know it. Please to go on, Mr So-and So.'

Though he sat between Lord Lincoln and the awesomely gifted Gladstone at these classes, Tupper was not in the least intimidated. It grieved him that he could not shine in ordinary conversation and he was the butt of some cruel jokes outside Biscoe's lecture rooms; on the other hand, he knew himself to be as good as any man at his studies. What was more, when it came to antecedents, he held what he considered to be an ace. The Tuppers were descended from German Protestants called Topfer, exiled from the Holy

Roman Empire by Charles V for their religious opinions and since scattered in Holland, Guernsey, England and – via the Founding Fathers – America. Always fond of improving a story, Tupper liked to believe that a Topfer had been one of Martin Luther's closest lieutenants. This gave him what he called his 'martyr's blood' and explained the sturdiness of his 'indignant Protestantism'. Such a man was not born to defer to mere temporal title.

Tupper was a Londoner. Born in 1810, he was the eldest of a family of five boys. His father was a popular and respected doctor with a house and practice in New Burlington Street, which extends from Regent's Street to Savile Row. Dr Tupper attended many aristocratic patients and early on his suavity of manner caught the eye of such as Lord Liverpool and the Duke of Wellington. He was a Guernseyman, and that branch of the family had recently provided many distinguished soldiers and sailors. A pleasing whiff of gunpowder hung over the name. There were American Tuppers who had fought on both sides at Bunker Hill.

Tupper's mother was the beautiful and talented

Ellin Devis, the niece of one painter and the daughter of another. There were green fields in her background – she was born in Lincolnshire and stood to inherit from her aunt Albury House, a fine property in rural Surrey. Neither she nor her husband were specially devout, nor were they among the more outrageous fashionables: they performed that difficult trick of being agreeable to everyone whilst concealing their deeper selves. Martin, their first-born, was an example of the child who turns out unexpectedly.

Until he went to Charterhouse, aged 11, he was an unhappy boy, but no more so than most who were pounded into shape by the schools and tutors of the era. The nicest thing he could remember happening to him was that George III once patted him affectionately on the head at Bognor. The adult Tupper liked to suppose that this was in one of the King's 'more lucid intervals'. Then again, maybe not: at the time of this benediction His Majesty's mental fog was almost complete and he could barely see further than the end of his nose.

When Tupper went up to Christ Church in 1828, he joined what he thought of as his rightful milieu. It was the age of improving and quasi-ecstatic under-graduate friendships, of long walks in the fields with a cherished companion, perhaps along the river to Iffley or up the London road to the quarries about Headington.

With two men like Tupper and Gladstone, the topic of conversation was more often than not the question of what God intended them to be. They were both old-fashioned Tories in temperament and evangelical by conviction. Their calling, as they saw it, was the Church. Pusey and Newman were high-minded Oxford examples: Newman, with his old-maid disdain of ordinariness and vulgarity, Pusey with his rare seraphic smile, which godliness told him to practise only on children.

Perhaps Gladstone saw more clearly than his friend the intellectual challenge that would follow ordination, but then, as well as being the cleverer of the two, he was also the most agonised. Tupper treated him fondly. He had succeeded over his friend in a small college prize put up by the Professor of Divinity – something he naturally liked to remember in later years, with the embellishment that Dr Burton had asked him to remit Gladstone a little of the money for coming such a plucky second. This was a very small academic blip, for Gladstone was one way or another headed for glory. If he did not always seem pleased by the idea, that only made him the more lovable. It made him, in the language of the day, a saint.

Though there was anguish and sometimes petulance in 'dear good Glad', in Tupper there was none. All he ever wanted was to be ordained a country parson. He had plenty of the hearty goodness that went along with what he imagined as pastoral duties, and he was a born sermoniser. One of the striking things about him was his fondness for argument by analogy. A mountain is composed of atoms. Without some binding power it will turn to dust, just as surely as will a man without faith. In another example, an earthquake throws up a barren reef. Soon enough lichens fasten on it and a cycle of life begins. Birds drop their seeds and so on, and the rock is fertilised. Tupper imagined even drowned sailors adding to the compost, until eventually the landscape resembled something akin to the path to Iffley, leafy and lovely. However, should the barren rock boast to the world of its fertility? Not at all: it was only fertile because of these very necessary additions and improvements. So it was with the mind of man when contemplating Holy Writ.

While Oxford and Christ Church undoubtedly egged Tupper on, he already thought like this. The clue to his whole life lay in some startlingly precocious verses he had written to his fiancée before he ever arrived at University.

Isabelle 'Issy' Devis was his cousin, a placid girl his own age with a long nose, dark hair and a rather sad smile. Her father was the painter Arthur William Devis, whose best known work was the *Death of Nelson*. Devis was an imprudent and unlucky man and the head of this branch of the family was not himself but a spinster aunt of Isabelle's. It was she who owned the large and rambling Albury House, located in the village of Albury, by the side of the Guildford-Dorking Road, which would one day come down to Tupper's mother. For a while, the old aunt turned the house into a school or academy for young ladies, while at the same time assuming a coat of arms and keeping up a town house in Marylebone.

When she died, William Devis was horrified to discover that the house on which he had set his hopes had never been intended for him in the first place.

As for Isabelle, her father died of apoplexy in 1822, leaving his family poor enough to issue lithographed appeals in the hope of securing a pension for his widow and an education for his daughter. Nothing much came of this. Isabelle was doomed to be the poor relation of the family.

She seems to have been plain and unassuming to a fault. Seen from her point of view, Martin Tupper was the eldest of five sons belonging to a rich and successful London doctor. It was wonderful that a boy from such a well-positioned family should take an affectionate interest in her, the country mouse. One day Albury House, which had figured so large in her life as a place to envy and admire, would be his. Before going up to Oxford, as a token of his feelings and to seal an engagement that was to last seven years, he wrote her this:

Seek a good wife of thy God, for she is the best gift of His providence;

Thou knowest not His good will: – be thy prayer then
submissive thereunto;
And leave thy petition to His mercy, assured that he will
deal with thee.

This was pretty remarkable for a 15-year-old
schoolboy, even one from Charterhouse. Its literary
sources were clear enough to anyone with even a nod-
ding acquaintance with the Bible. The poem, which
was destined to have such a profound effect on them
both, contained lines the startled Isabelle may have
taken a more blushing pleasure in:

Oh happy lot and hallowed, even as the joy of angels,
When the golden chain of godliness is entwined with the
roses of love.

No one else in the family spoke or thought in such
a tone. Isabelle was touched and flattered by the
poem – indeed she was quite bowled over by it. For a
young boy with what seemed like an incurable stammer, here was great and unexpected self-possession,
as well as strength of character and a precociously

settled mind. Moreover, tucked away as she was in Surrey with a widowed mother and no money, while her prospects of finding anyone else were not impossible, they were not good. Fifteen, a little on the plump side and not in the slightest bit intellectual, she settled down to wait.

Tupper came down from Oxford in 1832 with all his principles intact but no means of making a living. His friend Gladstone had accepted an offer from the Duke of Newcastle to represent the parliamentary seat of Newark. Tupper was disappointed that the Church had lost a notable double first but accepted that Gladstone had gone to the Commons in a great cause. As for himself, he accepted that he too would never be a parson. The stammer saw to that. Back in London, he experimented with foregoing meat for a while, subsisting on wedges cut from an enormous Cheshire cheese. It merely made him sick. He then attacked his speech impediment in a more direct way, much as it might have been a club-foot or a wasted arm. Dr Tupper narrowly prevented his son from undergoing surgery, proposed by some quack who wanted to cut away one or more of the 13 muscles of the mouth. He ended up doctoring himself with a not much less grotesque therapy. With a crutch jammed under his jaw and his tongue tied down, he set about reciting the whole of *Paradise Lost* and *Paradise Regained*. It did not work any better than the diet of cheese.

His father persuaded him to read for the bar, where his intelligence could be put to use and a career planned. But only a short while after entering chambers, he found the law bored him. He wrote to Gladstone in 1833 about much more apocalyptic matters.

> We live in a day of trouble, men's heart's failing them for fear, nation against nation and kingdom against kingdom – and the tide of public opinion roaring 'Where is the promise of His coming?', together with the tottering of governments, the national expectation of the Jews, the alarming crisis at which civilized society finds itself and other tongues speak in no unintelligible tongue, the time of the end...

This was perhaps too overheated a view of things for Gladstone to take to heart as a young MP. He was much more likely to have mentioned Tupper's name in connection with an incident that occurred when the Duke of Wellington passed on horseback through Lincoln's Inn Fields, surrounded by an angry mob of agitators. Tupper ran down from his chambers, jumped up on to some steps and yelped out 'Waterloo! Waterloo!', at which the jeers turned to just as noisy cheering. The Iron Duke tipped the young patriot a laconic salute, two fingers to the brim of his hat.

On 26 November 1835, the day after passing his bar examinations, Tupper married Isabelle. His father gave him £10,000, from which he could derive a modest but sufficient income of about £300 a year, and invited the newly-weds to live with him in the family house in Burlington Street. Here, nine months and a few days later, Issy gave the young lawyer a daughter, Ellin Isabelle. In 1837 they moved to a fairly substantial 'cottage' in the gothic style, a funny little house in St Pancras that had views over a distant Regent's

Park. A second daughter was born there in March 1838. He had no work as a lawyer but could afford to live in respectable if faintly anguished indolence. Then, suddenly, Tupper found what he could do in life.

It came about in a characteristic Tupperish way. He worshipped each week at Hampstead Road Chapel, a brisk walk away on the far side of the new Euston rail terminus, which had partially displaced the market gardens that he could see from his upstairs windows. The incumbent of the Hampstead Road Chapel was the Reverend Dr Henry Stebbings, a fine devout man who had the honour to be a former editor of the *Athenaeum*. In August 1837 Stebbings filled the tedium of a summer's afternoon in London by going to see the most loyal member of his congregation. He found Tupper at a loose end and, by way of encouragement, asked whether his young friend had anything that might do for the *Athenaeum*, or perhaps some other journal. After he had left, Tupper suddenly remembered the verses he had given to Issy ten years earlier. She ran to fetch them. A few days later he took them over to Hampstead Road.

The bookish Stebbings was mildly impressed and suggested various ways of trying to place them. Even while he was talking, Tupper felt the irresistible tug of a much greater idea. He would turn the few lines he had written Isabelle into a book, a whole book. Taking his leave of Stebbings as soon as he decently could, he rushed out into the street and – 'as I recollect, at the street corner post opposite Hampstead Road Chapel' – took out a pencil and began scribbling the opening lines of the work that was to change his life. Ignoring the passers-by and the smell of horse piss on the cobbles, he wrote, without a single crossing out or alteration, what his book would be about. It would feature:

> Thoughts that have tarried in my mind, and peopled its inner chambers,
> The sober children of reason, or desultory chain of fancy;
> Clear-running wine of conviction, with the scum and the lees of speculation;
> Corn from the sheaves of science, with stubble from mine own garner...'

In ten weeks, working at home and in his chambers at Lincoln's Inn, he turned out 250 pages of highly idiosyncratic verse – rambling, discursive but above all gloriously unshadowed by doubt and uncertainty.

The work was divided into 40 sections – 'Of Estimating Character', 'Of Cruelty to Animals', as well as more obvious musings on 'Love', 'Marriage', 'Education' and the like. The effect of it all was like being addressed by an old man with a white beard just outside some hermetic dwelling in the woods, a persona that seemed to fit the 27-year-old Tupper like a second skin. He chastened, he encouraged, he found sermons in stones and divine purpose in everything. From time to time, the text even approximates to a self-improvement book for those unlucky enough not to have studied at Oxford:

Reflection is a flower of the mind, giving out wholesome fragrance
But reverie is the same flower, when rank and running to seed.
Better to read little with thought, than much with levity and quickness...

In another passage, he talks about letter writing –

'the blessings poured upon the earth from the pen of a ready writer'. His advice is to write more:

> For a letter, timely writ, is a rivet to the chain of affection,
> And a letter, untimely delayed, is as rust to the solder.

Stebbings had given Tupper the name of a printer-publisher called Joseph Rickerby, who had offices on the first floor of a house in Sherbourn Lane, between Cannon Street and King William IV Street in the City. One short November day, Tupper bounded up the stairs determined not to take no for an answer. What might have weighed with him and given him encouragement was that Rickerby's premises were hard by the Wren edifice of St Mary's Abchurch, from which surely some goodness of heart must have leaked over the years. Rickerby inspected the contents of the parcel he had been given, scratched his ear, and agreed to publish at his own risk, he and the author to share any profits. The title of the work was agreed between them – it would be called 'Proverbial Philosophy'.

II

Tupper's book was published in January 1838, after the accession but before the coronation of Victoria. To everyone's surprise, the country had survived the Reform Act of 1832 without the world coming down about its ears. Moreover, in a few brief months Victoria had rekindled something Tupper had not seen in his lifetime – a respect and enthusiasm for royalty. The Queen's first public engagement was at the Lord Mayor's Banquet, in November 1837. The notoriously fickle London mob turned out to give her a gratifyingly warm welcome. She further pleased them by insisting on early occupation of the newly built but untenanted Buckingham Palace, ignoring the objections of her Household who pleaded it could not be got ready in time. Her deceptively strong will and occasional outbursts of temper in matters like this were surprising. The Tories, who wished to represent her as being the mere puppet of Lord

Melbourne and the Whigs, were slowly being forced to alter their tune. At 18, the first Queen for 153 years was absurdly young: it soon became clear that she was also extremely diligent and by no means a cypher.

In this bracing yet uncertain new climate more than one reviewer found *Proverbial Philosophy* disappointing. The most sympathetic notice came from Leigh Hunt, then in his fifties. This was a voice from another age, for Hunt had been a friend to Shelley and Keats – as well as Byron's enemy. Though he was everything that the cosmic Tory in Tupper deplored, Hunt was nevertheless the son of a preacher and he exercised his habitual kindliness on a work that 'strongly excites our curiosity, not by a certain quaintness of Scripture-referring expression (which, with all our respect for its conscientiousness is hardly natural to the time or indicative of sufficient prospective universality) but the manifest abundance, grace and benignity of its reflections.' Hunt – another childhood stammerer – was responding across the generational divide to gifts he once possessed himself.

The *Sunday Times* saw it as a religious book –

'a spirit, scriptural and unworldly, breathes through it' – and this was pleasing to Tupper but, from the point of view of potential sales, only a lukewarm endorsement. What sort of a book was it, then? Nobody could be sure. Given the speed of its composition, it is doubtful if Tupper himself knew what he was trying to say, although he was rattled to see the *Athenaeum* pooh-pooh the work as unlikely 'to please beyond the circle of a few minds as eccentric as the author's'. He thought – though he was mistaken – there was a whiff of Stebbings' professional jealousy here.

Proverbial Philosophy, a ragbag series of poetical subjects composed in such elevated haste, was proving to be a very stiff read. It suffered from the tyro's common mistake of trying to muffle up the easy and the obvious in a cloak of art. Even in an age accustomed to sermons, Hunt was right: the language was a stumbling block. The early Victorian world was filled with homiletic literature, more or less intelligible – and sometimes none the less thought of for being dense and obscure. But what was the reader to make of this?

One drachma for a good book, and a thousand talents for
a true friend:
So standeth the market, where scarce is ever costly:
Yea, were the diamonds of Golconda common as shingles
on the shore,
A ripe apple would ransom kings before a shining stone:
And so, were a wholesome book as rare as an honest
friend,
To choose the book be mine: the friend let another take.

This is unexpected and to most people counter-
intuitive. Tupper may have been indicating a genuine
personal choice but it was rather a donnish way of
looking at men and books. A casual reader who
bought a copy of *Proverbial Philosophy* and settled
down with it for help and encouragement was soon
likely to look around him with uneasy caution. Was a
good book really better than a good wife, or a sound
business partner? If so, did he have enough good
books? Or, uncomfortable thought, was it possible to
have too many?

Seven lines later in the piece Tupper finally says
what he means, providing a motto that subsequently

decorated the top rail of many a Victorian library: 'For a good book is the best of friends, the same today and forever.'

Despite its faults, the reaction to *Proverbial Philosophy* was on the whole favourable and a second edition was called for. However, when Rickerby brought out a third, it failed, and the unsold stock was shipped to America. All new books walk a financial tightrope. Most plunge to an untimely death. In this case, by dumping the unsold copies on the Americans, Tupper was done a fantastic service, as events were to prove.

In June 1838 he attended Victoria's coronation, sitting in the half-light of Westminster Abbey and watching the candle flames reflected on hundreds of tiaras. He had been quick to send the Queen a presentation copy of *Proverbial Philosophy*, though she declined the honour of having the second edition dedicated to her. A shocked member of the Royal Household explained that it was never done for the Sovereign to accept a second edition. Tupper made amends for this faux pas with an extemporised sonnet on the Coronation scene itself. His sense of drama completely overwhelmed his common sense :

> Never again – till earth casts out her dead,
> And teeming ocean yields her rescued prey –
> A sight so full of hope, delight and dread,
> Thrilling and grand, as met thy view this day
> Mayst thou behold.

Like Gladstone, who also had a ticket for the Abbey, Tupper found the Coronation service magnificently uplifting. The Queen could have told him otherwise, for the clergy were nervous and under-rehearsed. When it came to the ruby ring of State, the Archbishop of Canterbury found it had been made to fit the fifth and not the fourth finger. He set about vigorously screwing it on like a plumber with a cross-threaded nut. Towards the end, the Bishop of Bath and Wells, partly as a consequence of having turned over two pages at once, directed the Queen and Lord Melbourne to the Confessor's Chapel, where, mystified, they found themselves alone with dozens of bottles of wine and many plates of sandwiches shamelessly arranged on the altar. Melbourne poured himself a glass and waited for the clerical gentlemen to sort themselves out.

Tupper burst out of the Abbey that day with a full heart, for he was convinced by now that he was a poet, a man of letters. He might not have a single overarching theme in the same way as, for example, Wordsworth, but what he had to give the world was the very thing that made his critics pause – his voice. His actual speaking voice had improved beyond measure. He had discovered a Tupperian cure for his stammer and wondered why he had not thought of it sooner. He simply prayed the impediment away. And glory of glories, it worked. Here he was, in his own modest way, a fully-fledged author with powers that could only improve and grow stronger. Noticing that Coleridge's *Christabel* was a very fine yarn, he set himself the task of writing a sequel. Why not? It seemed to him there was little he could not do.

A smith at the loom, and a weaver at the forge, were but sorry craftsmen;
And a ship that saileth on every wind never shall reach her port:

Yet there be thousands among men who heed not the lean-
ings of their talents,
But cutting against the grain, toil on to no good end.

Not Tupper. He was on the way to becoming that
ideal of Victoria's long reign: the god-fearing man
with earthly powers and ambitions. Though he still
believed the Whigs to be the ruination of the country,
he saw their political base waning. Soon he and
people like him – the old-fashioned and unquestioning Tories of an age just passed – would be back in
the saddle. Then the country would learn what
Englishness really meant. In 1840 he blustered, 'I am
deliberately of the opinion that the sun of Great
Britain is sinking fast, and that our decline and fall
will be attributable to Whig principles.' This is the
exaggeration of an impatient man, for in fact everything that Tupper saw about the new reign he liked,
especially the arrival on the scene of Prince Albert,
with whom he could easily identify. What else was the
Coburg Prince but a lately arrived Topfer, stern in
principle and various in gifts?

In other words, Tupper was as loyal and noisy an

Early Victorian as his sovereign could possibly have wished for. Publication had released, if it had not channelled, a torrent of energy. The consequence was an egotism he could not restrain. Gladstone had a letter from him at the end of 1842:

> I am rejoiced to tell you that literature thrives with me, and threatens to make me rich, as well as – pardon my folly – famous. My den is quite an author's retreat, and I have the gratification of finding my poor – very poor – services solicited unsought...

This is more than a few steps along the road towards being smug, a word that was then changing its ancient meaning. From indicating something merely neat and tidy, the sense shifted quite suddenly to indicate things that were complacent and comfortably self-regarding. One of Tupper's new acquaintances, Douglas Jerrold, a founding contributor to *Punch* (1841) was the first to use the word smug in this way. It suited Tupper exactly.

While he waited for his inheritance, Tupper had bought a small house in Brighton. The location is important: with a free choice in the matter, Tupper was positioning himself away from the hurly-burly of London and so, in his eyes, underlining his gentlemanly status. Despite all his pleasurable feelings about fame, he had no intention of risking his social position for it. It was in Brighton in October 1842 that Isabelle gave him the son he much desired.

That same happy day, he went for a stroll along the Marine Parade, felt the familiar poetic urge upon him and fumbled for a pencil. Even the long-suffering Issy must have blenched a little when he came back and showed her the opening lines of yet another sonnet.

Not slender is the triumph and the joy,
To know and feel that, for his father's sake,
The world will look with favour on my boy...

Like the vicar he never became, the poet Tupper's benign certainty shone on the world. And blessings to He who rules above, the world was becoming more and more amenable to the vision Martin Tupper had of it. The world, properly considered, was a well-ordered Victorian family parlour. Snug – and smug.

Literary London both attracted and repelled him. He left Rickerby and took the far more fashionable Hatchard as his publisher. There was hardly a public occasion that didn't call forth a newspaper sonnet from him, and he also experimented (unwisely) with the novel. Harrison Ainsworth, then at the height of his fame, had, like Tupper, thrown over a career in the law to become a writer and literary journalist. Ainsworth's weekly salon at Kensal Manor House was frequented by Dickens and Thackeray and this is probably where Tupper first met Douglas Jerrold. The magnet that drew all these men to the far side of Chelsea was not merely their host's open-handed hospitality, but the chance of work. Ainsworth had just begun an eponymous literary magazine that was to last 11 years. As anyone at Ainsworth's parties could have told Tupper – Dickens included – to be really successful in periodic publishing he would need to live in London, join a club or two, and dine out more frequently.

This was not at all Tupper's idea of how to go

about things. Though he was prolific, he was not a hack, nor did he have a hack's painful humility. Thackeray, who had been his junior at Charterhouse, was at this time writing to keep the wolf from the door, with a decent chunk of his correspondence comprised of begging letters to editors and publishers. Tupper was by comparision almost a dilettante. He did contribute to the first issue of *Ainsworth's Magazine*, a strange piece about manned flight. He imagined his grandson a hundred years hence standing on what was left of the white cliffs of Dover, waiting to receive the mail from Australia. This would be put into his hand by a bird-man of 'limp and lithe' appearance, who had made the 14,000 mile journey fortified by lozenges, each with the strength of a quart of London porter, and an asbestos handkerchief on which to blow his nose.

Ainsworth got George Cruikshank to illustrate the article and would no doubt have taken more in the same vein. But Tupper stayed resolutely on the South Coast. He knew he stood to inherit Albury House from his mother one day soon; meanwhile, his father was unfailingly generous and encouraging. Children kept coming – Issy gave him another two sons to add to Martin junior.

In 1845 he wrote to his old friend Gladstone, by now President of the Board of Trade and a Privy Councillor, in partial apology for trying to solicit from him some pleasant sinecure, if one could be found.

As I have heretofore vexed you about patronage, it is fit for me to state that my prospects of a modest *aurea mediocritas* have been realised: only that, with a perpetual increase of blessings in the way of children, a similar increase in other ways would always be expedient.

Though he had written and published three novels, the basis of his modest affluence lay in *Proverbial Philosophy*. Hatchard had brought out a fourth and fifth edition and in 1842, rather than publish additions piecemeal in Ainsworth's new magazine, Tupper sat down and wrote an entire second series, to be published as a book. Its introduction is a masterpiece of self-confidence, for this time the author really does jump out of the shadows and buttonhole the reader like some whiskery Wild Man of the Woods.

Come again, and greet me as a friend, fellow-pilgrim
upon life's high highway,
Leave awhile the hot and dusty road, to loiter in the green-
wood of Reflection.
Come unto my cool dim grotto, that is watered by the
rivulet of truth,
And over whose time-stained rock climb the fairy flowers
of content :
Here, upon this mossy bank of leisure fling thy load of
cares,
Taste my simple store, and rest one soothing hour.

In life, such an invitation would be alarming to a
degree. Tupper's characterisation of himself is farci-
cally removed from his real persona as a complacent
gentleman with a thickening waist and a fondness for
amateur archaeology, five children and at least two
houses. Even without the faintly gothic outlines
implied by the 'cool dim grotto' the one thing that is
missing in the Tupper landscape is any sense that he
might be overreaching himself.

Into the bubbling brook I dip my hermit shell;
Man receiveth as a cup, but Wisdom is the river.

When he writes like this, you wonder who he had as ideal reader. It seems impossible that a public which had Dickens and Thackeray to entertain it, which could be so casually savaged by George Cruikshank's illustrations, could abide Tupper and his hermit cell. *Punch* was on to him early:

> Come along old fellow; follow me as a friend from the midnight streets:
> Leave awhile the cold and muddy Strand, to loiter in the tavern of the Coal-Hole.
> Come into this quiet box, with hot-water in a batter'd pewter jug,
> Over whose beer-stain'd table are strewn many particles of crust...

Thackeray, who drank at the Coal-Hole, may have been exasperated enough to have written this, niggled by what makes Tupper so infuriating to a modern ear – the shamelessness of his stance:

> I roam no heath-empurpled hills, wearily watching for a covey,
> But thoughts fly swift to my decoy, eager to be caught...

I chase no solitary stag, tracking it with breathless toil,
But hunt with Aureng-Zebe, and spear surrounded thousands.

Yet part of his appeal was that there was no one else quite like him. From the point of view of novelty, a sought-after quality in any age, Mr Martin Tupper scored heavily. If what he said didn't always make sense, that was acceptable too. The way he said it flattered a readership looking for devotional exercise but just as hungry for dramatic expression. There was always thunder and lightning in Tupper, as well as bugles, crashing waves and celestial choirs. He was noisy.

What he did not possess was that spirit of ribaldry the ephemeral press of the day so delighted in, its taste for bad puns and schoolboy facetiousness. The problem with his bird-man fantasy was that he half believed it possible: what might have seemed merely ridiculous to Ainsworth lingered in Tupper as prophetic utterance. He was bad on froth. He had a vicar's clumsy ability to romp but was strangled by an underlying earnestness.

In the early years of her reign, Victoria relied heavily on Lord Melbourne for advice. The cynic in him was flattered. 'You had better try to do no good,' he drawled to her once, when she was taking her first steps in statecraft 'and then you'll get into no scrapes.' It was deliciously wicked, this sort of thing, but it did not last. By 1842 Melbourne was out and the person who replaced him as adviser was not another Prime Minister, but Prince Albert. And there was a faint resemblance to Tupper in the Prince Consort, with his hearty and humourless protestantism, his lack of a full self-awareness and an embarrassingly obvious libido. Albert, too, had a marked fondness for improving the shining hour by platitudes.

The strange thing was – and it helps place Tupper more accurately – the Prince easily beat down his critics. Try as they might, the satirists could not prick him. He made an ass of himself over many things ('Ben Lomond wears a lofty aspect today,

Sire.' Albert, slowly and with Germanic suspicion, 'Benjamin who?') but he was determined enough to be feared as well as ridiculed. There was an air of dogged invincibility about the Prince. Tupper felt the same way about himself. He was an oddity but a powerful one.

With the creation of the second series of *Proverbial Philosophy*, Tupper found himself stroking a very willing cat. *PP*, as he described it in letters, was the publishing phenomenon of the 19th century. By 1880 there would be 50 editions of this preposterous book, which had no narrative, no incidental characters other than himself, and which was written in a sort of gluey English that had no equivalent in ordinary speech. The worthy and pious John Hatchard had a grandson who was an ordained minister and he knew a little about the English taste for moralising. Before his death in 1846, the venerable publisher made a point of congratulating his author. Patting him on the head, he said 'When your hair is as white as mine, you will have cause to thank this book of yours.'

He was right. *PP* never sold less than 5,000 copies

a year for nearly 80 years, from 1838 right through to the First World War. Its total sales, in Britain and America, are calculated to have been not less than a million and a half. After 1842 not a line was changed, not so much as a semicolon altered. It was a text that apparently needed no revision. Men who had read it in their youth bought it for the marriage of their children and later gave it as a worthwhile coming of age present to their grandchildren. It was like a trick candle, inextinguishable.

Old Dr Tupper died in 1844; his wife three years later. Thanks to friendships enjoyed by his father, Tupper was made a Fellow of the Royal Society, then open to anyone 'eminently distinguished in one of the learned professions'. The Duke of Argyll and the Marquis of Bristol – former patients of Dr Tupper – were among those who stood as sponsors. There was more to come. In 1847, the year he inherited Albury House, Tupper was made Doctor of Common Law at Oxford, admission to which required him to sit for three hours, waiting to rebut (in Latin) anyone who wished to contest the candidature. While he waited, he composed a celebratory sonnet.

These titles were hardly gewgaws; they add another telling detail to his portrait. It is difficult for example to imagine Thomas Carlyle as F. R. S. – when in his extreme old age Bismarck arranged for the historian to receive the Prussian Order of Merit, Carlyle said with characteristic grumpiness that he would have preferred a quarter pound of tobacco. This was 30 years after Tupper had accepted with unbecoming alacrity a Gold Medal for Science and Literature from the King of Prussia, who had studied *Proverbial Philosophy* with pleasure and, he said, instruction.

Tupper's minor poetic output – his newspaper musings – continued like the most reliable kind of fountain, or perhaps in a better image, a watchman's comforting chant. Few public events passed without his versified reflections – he felt he was doing the Poet Laureate's job for him. In a way, he was. Odes succeeded sonnets; hymns were piled on prose. If what he had to say was sometimes banal, if its manner infuriated far better poets, he could aways point to the amazing popularity of *Proverbial Philosophy*. Tupper intended the world should understand something from its study of *PP*, something that stood outside the text: no matter how facile his pen, the author was not a scribbler. He was a Christian gentleman.

In 1845, he entered into an agreement with a Mr Herman Hooker, of Philadelphia, giving him exclusive rights to publish both series of *Proverbial*

Philosophy in America. The legal papers were drawn up by Tupper in Brighton and solemnly decorated with the family seal. The honest Hooker paid him $3,000 (£80), the most Tupper was ever to earn in America. This mattered less than the fame, which promised – on that side of the Atlantic even more so than in England – to be everlasting. (And indeed the last American edition was printed over a hundred years later, in the days of the Korean war and the Macarthy witch-hunts, long after Tupper was completely forgotten in his own country).

With his usual ebullience, he set out to discover the basis of his American reputation. He found his work had been energetically taken up in the States by a journalist called Nathaniel Parker Willis, who was only four years older than Tupper himself. Willis had been labouring under the pleasant delusion that he had discovered for the American public a hitherto unknown Elizabethan poet. When he came to London on a visit in 1845, he was astonished when this contemporary of Shakespeare and Bacon sent in a card to his lodgings:

I called on Mr Tupper the next day with some curiosity –
picturing to myself a grey-headed patriarch, and preparing myself to treat him with proper reverence, and express
very gratefully my sense of the honour of his visit. I was
shown into a very elegant library of well thumbed books
by a servant in mourning livery, and after employing
myself a few minutes in looking at the statuary and other
marks of taste around me, enter – a very young man with
black curling locks, twenty seven at the utmost, ruddy and
handsome, and with a manner boyishly cordial!

Tupper was actually 35, but this was a detail. The
journalist had a good human interest story on his
hands that he did not intend to let slip. His subject
was, to begin with, so frank and jolly. The universality he strove for was perceived by Willis as democratis-
ing zeal. Even his patriotism was appealing: here was
a man who loved his country in a way an American
could understand. Willis may not have explained to
his interviewee that the undertaking entered into with
Hooker, which Tupper intended to be a prototype
for a copyright agreement that did not come into
existence between the two countries until 1891, was
not worth the paper it was written on. Tupper was

already being ripped off by almost anyone with a newspaper to fill – N.P. Willis of the *Evening Mirror* included.

What America had to offer him was glory. What it could not give him were royalties. He found this out all too quickly – his three novels were packaged up by one heartless pirate and sold at 37 cents for the set. As for the deal with Hooker, three years after Tupper's exclusive agreement with him there were five competing editions of *Proverbial Philosophy* available at knock-down prices. One publisher, the firm of Wiley and Putnam, had it in ten different formats. You could read it in a cheap edition for next to nothing, and for a few cents more you could have it in a de luxe binding to put next to your Bible.

Tupper would have been inhuman not to respond to the blandishments of his American readership. In 1849, in place of hard cash, he received a love token which was said to have come from fifty thousand ecstatic readers of the Ladies Repository. What he wanted from his American public was just what they were most anxious to give him, love and respect. In many ways, he was by now everything he ever wished to be as a parson, only with an immense parish. The admiration of visiting American luminaries delighted him. One of them, J.C. Richmond, wrote to him from Oxford: 'I was in the midst of the colleges and if I read your ballad once at Exeter at dinner, I read it as well in Merton, Oriel and the rest... I dined in Xt Ch. with your friend the Rev. W. E. Jelf and all were rejoiced and somewhat amazed at yr great popularity in the U. States.'

This is very easy to believe. Jelf, a contemporary of Tupper's at Christ Church, was a fine scholar but an irascible and unpopular man whose own hopes were pinned on his Greek Grammar, just published. The recital of Tupper's American fame was news he could have done without – he was just about to take up a living in the tiny mill-town of Carlton, up on the moors behind Skipton, in Yorkshire. But then the poet philosopher had already published a text that might suit Jelf's situation – one of the most popular poems he ever wrote:

Never give up! there are chances and changes
Helping the hopeful a hundred to one,

And through the chaos High Wisdom arranges
Ever success, if you'll only hope on :
Never give up! for the wisest is boldest,
Knowing that Providence mingles the cup,
And of all maxims the best as the oldest
Is the true watchword of Never give up!

In 1851, after being presented at Court by Gladstone and stifling the disappointment he felt at not being made Poet Laureate after the death of Wordsworth, Tupper turned his mind to the Great Exhibition. He composed a 'Hymn for All Nations' which was eventually entered as an exhibit. Deservedly so. The hymn was set to music by Dr Samuel Sebastian Wesley, the celebrated organist and natural son of the great hymnist. What made Tupper's hymn so remarkable was that the author managed to solicit 25 translations of it as a way of indicating the international scope of the Exhibition. The Headmaster of Shrewsbury School provided the Greek version, an assistant master at Eton the Latin. Dante Gabriel Rossetti's father obliged with an Italian translation. There was a Sanscrit version from a Cambridge don and – an inspired stroke of nonsense – from the caribou grazing lands of Canada the Chief of the Ogibwa Nation came up with a melancholy-rendering beginning:

Monedoo ke ween e gook
Noos ke de nah goo me gook.

Ever since Willis's visit and the publicity he gave to Tupper, fan mail from America had been pouring into the Albury post office. Mary Chase, of New York State and herself an author, gives the tone:

I was at the house of a neighbour six miles distant: he is a man of fifty, a rich, sour, miserly, uneducated, singularly uninteresting man. His house is a very small, ugly stone structure, containing the furniture his parents left him. I saw on the shelf a few old smoked-dried worthless volumes, an antique bible and a gay red-covered book that seemed quite out of place there. I took it down – it was soiled but not torn – there were no children in the old curmudgeon's house – it was 'Proverbial Philosophy'! To think that droll Nat Peckham, hateful and grim, should

ever buy that book! 'Why Nat where did this come from –
it ain't yours ?'

'Yes, tis, too, and there's more sense in that book than
any I ever saw, except the Bible.'

Was I not right in calling this Fame?

Tupper thought she was. There was a Tupper Lake
in Miss Chase's home state, named after a pioneer
forebear who may have been no more appetising in his
day than Nat Peckham of Columbia County. Yet
where was the virtue in finding and naming a mere
sheet of water, compared to the redemptive power of
words that could rescue some singularly uninteresting
old fool from his ignorance and sloth? Moreover,
however solitary a backwoodsman he was, Nat
Peckham was sure to have read Tupper's address to
the thirteenth President of the United States, reprint-
ed in all or almost all of the 1,400 newspapers of the
continent. 'I admire it very much for its great wisdom, and its publication in so many of our newspapers is no small proof of its merit,' President Fillmore
declared handsomely.

Fanny Trollope said of her trip to America in the

late 1820s that the continent 'was hardly better known than Fairy Land; and the American character has not been much more studied than that of the Anthropopagi; all therefore was new, and everything amusing.' She was writing from Cincinnati, or 'Porkopolis', where the hogs ran wild in the street and ate up the garbage before being taken back to their pens and butchered. That last adjective in Fanny Trollope's remark was the dangerous one: the Republic might be crude and tough but did not set out its stall to be amusing.

The visit of Dickens ten years later started off much better but ended badly. There was a huge appetite for European celebrity in America, which at first Dickens enjoyed satisfying. Hundreds of people queued to shake him by the hand in every hotel he stayed at and because his movements were such a matter of interest to the press, if he looked out of the window from a train, it was to see someone – sometimes hundreds of unknown well-wishers – waving from the track-side. He was asked a lot of silly questions and shown a great too many asylums and prisons but in general his hosts could hardly have been more hospitable. The country felt it had done him proud, and was justifiably outraged when the briskly sniping *American Notes* was published.

Lack of copyright caused the bad feeling. Dickens was famous in America, but like Tupper he was also being robbed blind. The full title of the book he wrote was an indication of the problem – *American Notes for General Circulation*. He had to be restrained by Forster from adding this epigraph, taken from the transcript of a recent Old Bailey trial:

> In reply to a question from the Bench, the Solicitor for the Bank observed that this kind of notes circulated the most extensively in those parts of the world where they were stolen and forged.

Dickens was young – he celebrated his thirtieth birthday on the train from Worcester to Springfield, Massachusetts. Youthful or not, the Americans found his combative side hard to take and misread his incurably sardonic manner as arrogance and a contempt for their institutions. The copyright quarrel, which he ventilated in two public speeches, seemed to them the complaints of a greedy and ignorant man. They had expected better.

He was just as disappointed in them. He wrote to the actor William Macready,

> this is not the Republic of my imagination... the man who comes to this country a Radical and goes home again with his old opinions unchanged, must be a Radical on reason, sympathy, and reflection, and one who has so well considered the subject, that he has no chance of wavering.

Before going himself, Tupper sought out his greatest contemporary, or says he did. He would have found Dickens completely unrepentant. There was a healthy paradox here. Tupper was no democrat, yet Willis had been right about him – his godliness and love of his own country chimed with things Americans held dear. Talking to Dickens in London he may have struck a sorry, even a preposterous figure. He was to turn out to be a far more reliable witness to what America was actually like.

Dickens started out in Boston; Fanny Trollope at the mouth of the Mississipi. Tupper landed at New York in 1851 and was taken straight from the docks to the editorial offices of the *New York Evening Post*. The editor and joint proprietor, William Cullen Bryant, immediately asked him for any musings he might have made on his journey over. Naturally, Tupper had some in his pocket. Bryant was delighted. This was the kind of man he could do business with. When his visitor went on to explain how he had been saved by Providence from a bizarre death, having been blown horizontal over the rail of the steamship Asia during a storm at sea, hanging on to life by his merest fingertips, Bryant liked that too.

Tupper pleased everybody he met. He in turn was entranced and found some of his native prejudices quickly overturned.

Singular to say, I find the Irish waiters everywhere uncommonly civil, useful and good sort of folks: and all middle and lower classes seem to have more frankness and less servility than ours over the water: they possibly would be impertinent if you were proud; but, if one's only free and easy, they really show one a vast deal of genuine kindness. I like them.

Bryant, as well as being something of a poet himself, was gate-keeper to the very rich. By his efforts, Tupper was dined by men like the ancient financier Samuel Bulkely Astor and the property developer Ruggles and his son-in-law Strong. He was taken by the Mayor of New York on a tour of its public institutions; enthusiastically fêted by the writer Washington Irving and the newspaper magnate Gordon Bennett. There was only one hiccup. At a dinner for 350 guests, Tupper attempted a mildly ingratiating joke. His throwaway remark, 'I do not wish to write a book about you,' was misheard and at once someone jumped up and roared, 'Not in the Dickens style!'. Pandemonium followed. Tupper fell back into his chair in dismay as his hosts tried to restore order by repeated tooting on a hunting-horn. It was a close-run thing.

The sequel was telling. Gordon Bennett wrote an article in the *New York Herald* explaining how Tupper had been grievously misunderstood and the editor of the *Public Ledger* called in person to apologise. New York liked Martin Tupper, even when he declared, with his usual artless enthusiasm, that Americans 'deserve to be called Englishmen'. It was absurd, but it was better than having Dickens telling them they never could be.

He went next to Philadelphia. He shook hands with 200 young girls who were taking a public examination at a Ladies College. Later that day, he beguiled the members of a blind academy who gave him a giant braille scroll reading: 'A VISIT FROM MR TUPPER AFFORDS US GREAT PLEASURE.' They flocked about him with their hands brushing his clothes and face like gentle and affectionate bees. Many a European visitor had been tripped up by such organised visits to hospitals and asylums, prisons and schools. Tupper instinctively understood he was being shown pride in American achievement. In politics he was about as radical as a cucumber, but he could recognise worthiness when he met it. As the historian Elie Halevy later pointed out, American virtue was not a good in itself. It was only as good as it was useful.

Tupper was responding to something that seemed to some Europeans like a contradiction of purpose. For all its bustle and what he described as the country's 'mercantile fermentation', he recognised in his hosts a deep conservatism, an unwillingness to be budged from far older values, those to be found in family, hearth, church and a respect for the counsels of the old. It was a pity he had no intention of writing a book about America, for he was among the first to identify the idea of the moral majority.

The showcase event of his visit to Pennsylvania was a tour of the Hospital for the Insane. 'When Dr Kirkbride introduced me to them as the writer of their favourite book, many a wild eye looked lovingly on me and many a feverish hand squeezed mine with affection,' he wrote to Isabelle. This is Tupper at his best and most lovable. He was astounded to hear the patients recite his poem 'Never Give Up' and took it as an instance of their interest in good literature, until he realised that it was tacked to the back of every door in the building. Not a bit put out, he promised to send Kirkbride the music, for in England, as he assured him, 'Never Give Up' was already a very popular concert piece. Dr Kirkbride and the inmates cheered him to the rafters.

After a lightning visit to Canada, where in Kingston, Ontario, a young couple knocked at his hotel door and asked him to marry them (he refused, very regretfully), he went back to Washington, writing to the President to ask for the honour of an interview. Millard Fillmore immediately invited him to dinner at the White House.

There is no style or ceremony, [Tupper later recorded] or restraint in any way at the President's house or table, beyond what you would meet at every private dwelling. This was almost a state occasion, the cabinet dinner before the President's departure on some public errand northward; but all was ease, affability and absolute practical equality. The President is a portly, nice-looking, respectable man in black clothes and grey hair, well bred, affable, dignified and so kind and pleasant that it's impossible to be otherwise than quite at ease before him.

Mrs Fillmore and the President's son were a little on the quiet side, but his daughter played the piano for the company and then very graciously presented the music to Tupper for his own eldest daughter, Ellin. Dickens would have been a more formidable guest that night and Thackeray a wittier one, but Tupper had a sweet quality that charmed everybody he met. As the evening wound on, the members of Fillmore's cabinet left one by one, until he was alone with the Presidential family and, in some pleasant way that cannot be taught, at home with them.

Two days later, the British Ambassador, Sir Henry Bulwer, took him down to Baltimore to a speaking engagement at the Maryland Historical Society. Tupper probably spoke for far too long, and a Mr J. P. Kennedy, who followed him, tried to vary the tone a little by lightly denouncing authorship as 'an idle craft'. It was an after-dinner pleasantry but the audience was surprised when Tupper jumped up a second time.

'Authorship', he told his hosts, 'is an impulse – a thing a man cannot help. We write because there is something in us which must come out.' It was as succinct a statement as he ever made about his literary life – and it has the ring of truth. The company took it in exactly that light.

Cincinnati begged him to visit, but it was hot and he was finding that life on the road was hard work. In Pittsburgh, he sat sweating in his hotel room, suffering from the petulance that overcomes all touring authors. Isabelle, who had heard of so many wondrous receptions and banquets, might have been startled to have received this letter:

> Fifty times a day I have rejoiced that none of you, wife and babes, are with me: it would utterly have knocked you all up; and you would have been unspeakably miserable both at inns and in travelling conveyances... [A]ll the country is rough, uncleared, and uncomfortable living: nearly all the houses of wood, roof and all; hot in summer and cold in winter; stumps by thousands in every field; and the dense jungle everywhere in the rear; roads horrible; country towns dirty, straggling, shabby.

Cincinnati and the sirens of the Ladies Repository called in vain – Tupper retreated to Philadelphia and thence to New York. He ended his American tour at

Castle Garden, where Jenny Lind was giving a concert. The promoter and impresario Barnum sought him out in the sea of faces and took him backstage to meet the singer. The Swedish Nightingale had of course been presented with her copy of *Proverbial Philosophy* long ago and now she sat holding Tupper's hand and crying with emotion while the management of the theatre frantically tried to get her on stage for a bow.

'I was quite sorry to leave her,' he wrote to Isabelle, 'and when, putting aside all idle musical compliments, I tried to cheer her up by the thought how nobly and generously for many good purposes she was using the melodious gift of God to her, poor Jenny only looked up devoutly, shook her head and sighed, and seemed unhappy.'

The singer was halfway through a two-year tour, in which Barnum dragged her across America and back, earning her £20,000. As she well knew, three days later Tupper was off back to England, the bosom of his family and the tamed beauties of the Surrey countryside. That might have accounted for her tears.

IV

When he walked up the drive to Albury House at the end of May 1851, it was to reunite with a family that had grown to eight children; the youngest of them, Alice, not yet two years old. For someone so recently fêted in the White House, his own domestic circumstances came as something of a shock. The most pressing business was to find a way of extending the accommodation. To celebrate his return, Tupper commissioned an architect to add a wing to the house. It was a pleasant way of indicating to his Surrey neighbours that the friend of Millard Fillmore and the toast of New York was a man of substance.

Such a numerous family was the embodiment of an Early Victorian ideal, the Royal marriage pointing the way. Queen Victoria was married on 10 February 1840 and woke up with morning sickness five weeks later. By 1851 there were seven royal children. Their mother was still only 32 years old and would be confined twice more before she was forty. The Queen's capacity for child-bearing was not so much remarked upon in the comic press as was her general unhealthy doting upon 'the German sausage-maker', the Prince who gave her such regular pregnancies. *Punch* did wonder briefly in 1844 what the situation would be in 1860, representing the Queen as a familiar nursery-rhyme figure – 'There was a royal lady who lived in a shoe, etc.' The cartoon was drawn by Leech, a contemporary of Tupper's at Charterhouse who came down to Albury from time to time for the fishing.

Most Victorians would have counted Leech's drawing (in which an absurdly youthful Victoria flourishes a bundle of birch twigs over a tribe of children numbering 20 or more) something of a cheap shot. A large family was not a cause for censure and nobody with any taste looked beyond the nursery to the secrets of the marriage bed. John Leech (who had only two children) would have found no local sniggering about the Albury House tribe of Tuppers when he came to visit. As far as the villagers were concerned, they had a notably worthy neighbour among them, as indicated by the number of distinguished strangers they directed to his gate. As well as the gentle giant Leech, with his rods and baskets, these included representatives of the Government of Liberia, memorable not simply by their colour and imposing girth, but also for their costume. They pitched up from the London-Guildford train one summer's morning wearing full court dress and sporting wonderfully polished beaver hats.

The owner of Albury House carried off the part of country gentleman to perfection. He was so frank, so roly-poly jolly, it was a pleasure to exchange the time of day with him. The village rejoiced in Mr Tupper as a staunch patriot, a loquacious ruralist and a decided friend to animals. He could speak Greek and Latin to the vicar and doggerel to the cottage children and old people he met along his way. He was that prized thing in country life, a man whose manners could be understood by anyone. As to what went on behind his doors, that was his own business. He was assumed, on the evidence of his writings, to be a model patriarch.

As with the Royal Household, Tupper's daughters

were much more of a solace to him than his sons. The eldest of these was a terrible disappointment. Martin Charles Selwyn Tupper, like Albert Edward, Prince of Wales, failed miserably to come up to snuff. A lanky, good-looking boy, he was sent to Winchester, where he idled and assumed all those schoolboy vices that had been such strangers to his father. He smoked, he gambled, and showed no interest in study. To please Tupper, a child had to be quick and bright, with an aptitude for verse. Young Tupper had none of these gifts and no desire to acquire them. He also drank.

So, it turned out, did his mother. This was much more serious. Issy did not have the intelligence and resourcefulness of, say, Gladstone's wife, a very beautiful woman who had an even harder early marriage. Catherine Gladstone was at first alarmed by and then resigned to her husband's relentless political ambition and moral rectitude, which went along with eight children in thirteen years. But then Mrs Gladstone had the consolations of fame and society which she enjoyed in her own right, as well as a far more substantial income. By comparison, Issy Tupper had the children and a quiet and semi-retired life in the country. Once, it would have been enough. Over time it became painfully apparent that Mrs Tupper was a very unhappy woman. By the 1850s, the household was augmented by a live-in nurse, provided by a mysterious outsider, Dr Sutherland.

This was the real secret of Albury House, which like all village secrets soon became common knowledge. Sutherland was a mad doctor and the word nurse a euphemistic term for attendant. Twice Tupper had been forced to send his wife away for short periods in an attempt to settle her mind and empty it of what he described as 'the terrible idea of evil possession'.

When he came back from his American triumphs, things were as bad with Issy as they possibly could be. Though he had written to her regularly, she seems to have been made frantic by jealousy, not of the sexual kind, but derived (as would have been clear to anyone other than Tupper) from a much more obvious source. While he was having all the fun, being romanced by the President of the United States and his family, she was stuck with the children, one of whom, little Alice, was extremely sickly. (She had a deformed spine and died the following year). Meanwhile, every action Issy took was either questioned or even more irritatingly commended by Dr Sutherland's watchful nurse.

It is clear from four letters Tupper wrote to Gladstone in 1853 how the problem manifested itself.

...It is not madness, but evil and perilous propensities. Well, this trouble, which I have borne secretly and to much misconstruction until her evils became notorious, – breeds others. Though I bear up bravely for my children's sake, their mother's conduct will lose them station, unless I gain advancements.

Gladstone was startled to learn that Issy had been profoundly depressed since 1848. She drank to keep the blue devils at bay. Because this particular falling off from virtue was more uncommon among women – that's to say middle-class women – the scandal was greater than it would have been if Tupper himself had been the drunk of the family. Issy's role, as it was perceived by society, was to provide a welcoming home and bed for her husband, but also to furnish a social ambiance for her daughters. Boys – like the wayward Martin Charles Selwyn – were expected to run wild. That was what schools were for, to tame them. Girls were largely educated at home. From about the age of 11, they were being prepared for marriage. Tupper took Issy's problem as a dereliction of duty towards the girls in particular. He wrote to Gladstone:

> That morbid affections, continually illustrated by frantic temper, frenzied jealousy and perpetual worry by night and by day have (now for some five years) made your Socratic friend the very martyr of marriage is a most unhappy truth: at the same time, I have managed so well, so patiently, and so cheerfully, – that the confession would surprise many of my not intimate friends. Moreover, – except when under the evil influence (which is too often excited by stimulants when she can get at them) – no one would suspect the poor penitent creature of such wicked capabilities: and frequently, especially with strangers, she is all that one could wish her to be.

This is ugly and painful to read. Tupper was not writing to his friend for advice on how to help Issy, nor as a means of examining his own contribution to her problems. What he wanted from Gladstone was some kind of government sinecure, something on the pension list that would help him defray the medical costs of keeping her at home. The year after the letters, baby Alice died. Much more poignantly, Issy, evil and possessed or not, miscarried her ninth child.

Gladstone did ask Lord Aberdeen briefly if anything could be done for Tupper, but there the matter ended. Gladstone considered his Oxford friend had been perfectly right to ask the political favour but anything else was out of the question. Both men understood this. Issy Tupper may have been included in Gladstone's prayers, which were wide-ranging enough to include sinners of all complexion, but it would not have done to interfere in any more practical way. In fact, it would have been as embarrassing as the sin itself.

Issy was one of a vast army of Victorian women who, it was thought, would do better by getting on with the job than complaining about it. It was a woman's duty to promote her husband's happiness, even at the expense of her own. If there was some other way of looking at family life, Tupper did not know of it. The gardener looked after the garden, the housewife looked after the house. As for anything else, *Proverbial Philosophy* had the answer:

Helps invisible but real, and ministerings not unfelt,
Angelic aid with worldly discomfiture, bodily loss with the soul's gain,
Secret griefs, and silent joys, thorns in the flesh, and cordials for the spirit
(– Short of the insuperable barrier dividing innocence from guilt –)
Go far to level all things, by the gracious rule of Compensation.

In the end, Issy cured herself. By the time she was beyond childbearing and her existing children were grown up, she could see her husband more clearly for what he was. He was still the 15-year-old boy who had proposed to her in the garden at Albury, the precocious but essentially unimaginative child whose goddess was not love, but fame. He was kind, he was insufferably priggish – and he was stupid. She might be the only person in the country to think him that but it was her one piece of learning. 'The insuperable barrier that divided innocence from guilt,' was a phrase that read well but bore little relationship to daily life. If the Albury House cook craftily set aside a cut of meat for her old mother; if a maid scooped up a penny or two left carelessly by one of the boys; if the gardener said he was at work on Saturday when he wasn't, had an insuperable barrier been crossed? In the same way, if Issy was driven mad by loneliness and insecurity, enough to steal the great poet's sherry, then was that guilt or self-preservation?

Isabelle Tupper had discovered a sad truth. As many a wayward family member had realised, both in Britain and America, *Proverbial Philosophy* was a useless set of doctrines when it came down to it. Its author knew a lot about the art of homily but nothing at all about life.

Face thy foe in the field, and perchance thou wilt meet thy master,
For the sword is chained to his wrist, and his armour buckled for the battle;
But find him when he looketh not for thee, aim between the joints of his harness,

And the crest of his pride will be humbled, his cruelty will bite the dust.

It is doubtful if Tupper ever knew exactly what he was advising in lines like this. When they were acted upon to the letter by the sepoys who precipitated the Indian Mutiny, the unmanliness and cunning of the mutineers disgusted and outraged the whole nation. Issy may have been the first to see through her husband: it saved her sanity to realise he could be wrong and more often than not was speaking for the sake of it. Instead of fighting him, she accepted the part of his personality she could cope with, that of the faintly Pickwickian fool who only wanted everyone to be as happy as he was himself.

Between 1850 and 1860, 28 further editions of *Proverbial Philosophy* were published. If one were to multiply the number of copies sold by five to make a guess at the readership, it seems there was hardly a home in England that had not heard something of the book. One of Tupper's correspondents was a convict who wrote from a drippingly dank cell in Dartmoor prison. Another was Leopold, King of the Belgians. In 1854 a German edition of the work came out. For some reason the book also struck a chord in Armenia. Sweden and Denmark brought out translations. In America, copies multiplied like prairie gophers.

Tupper had taken pains to send his work not only to the Queen but to other key members of the Royal Household. Until her retirement in 1850, he had a particular friend at Court, Gladstone's mother-in-law, Lady Lyttleton, one of Victoria's ladies-in-waiting. *Proverbial Philosophy* duly found its way into the Royal nursery. A personal copy was held by Sarah Hildyard, the children's English teacher. Miss Hildyard was a vicar's daughter whose special charge was Vicky, the Queen's eldest daughter, for whom she acted as governess. Miss Hildyard went some way to humanising the educational programme laid down for all the children by the Prince Consort and seems to have succeeded in charming the humourless tutor Frederick Gibbs, whose struggles with the petulant Prince of Wales were a feature of the nursery room.

In 1854, all the Royal tutors had the bright idea of preparing a masque to be performed by the children in honour of their parents' wedding anniversary. The theme was to be the four seasons and the text an adaptation of the poem by James Thomson. The designs were by the watercolourist Edward Corbould, who had been engaged by the Prince Consort as 'instructor of historical painting to the Royal Family'. Like Miss Hildyard, Corbould was a Tupper fan and together they hit on the idea of commissioning from their favourite poet some uplifting finale in his own style, to be performed by the eight-year-old Princess Helena. Tupper obliged almost by return of post. The production took the form of tableaux played behind a gauze screen. Princess Alice (eleven) came out first as Spring, scattering flowers and reciting her Thomson 'in a tone of voice sweet and penetrating like that of the Queen'. Summer was played by Vicky (fourteen) while her baby brother Arthur (four) slept under a sheaf of corn, the skimpiness of his little blue smock startling the Queen. (Miss Hildyard was at pains to whisper that he was wearing flesh-coloured tights). Autumn was signified by the ten-year-old Arthur as Bacchus, wearing a leopard skin and a crown of grapes. That rude and sulky boy the Prince of Wales, who was 13, played Winter, wearing preposterous icicle whiskers made from cardboard, while his companion Louise (six) was decked out in what the Prussian Ambassador's wife considered 'a sort of Russian dress' and sat before a fire of twigs. The Queen's *Journal* described the final tableau.

> The 5th and last one combined the four others, which had each been separately represented. In the Clouds, at the back, stood dear little Lenchen [Helena] reciting very pretty verses specially written for the purpose by Mr Martin Tupper, – as the spirit of the Empress Helena... We were all delighted and the whole was such a pretty idea.

The eight-year-old Helena, tricked out in a white veil that reached to her toes and carrying a long gilt crucifix, explained to the select audience that she was the Christ-loving Empress whose purpose was to bless this happy day. She concluded the show with these words from Tupper's pen:

With plenteous peace on these rejoicing shores
May God for England crown the coming year –
And pour new mercies from His heavenly stores
On Thee – and Thee – most honoured and most dear:

O Parents, happy in a home so blest
With subject's homage and with children's love –
May earth still shower upon you all that's best,
And more than best be yours in Heav'n above!

England declared war on Russia seven weeks later. Tupper, who had not been present at the masque of the seasons, dashed off a couple of patriotic poems: 'Away to the War has the Soldier departed' and a 'Dirge for the Czar'. He had received some complimentary letters from Sarah Hildyard and her colleague Gibbs, indicating the Queen's pleasure in his verses for Princess Helena and was therefore not surprised when Sarah Hildyard wrote suggesting he wrote something slight to honour the Queen's birthday, which was on 24 May. He had 20 days to come up with an idea. Once again he sent the text by return of post. The poem ended with an

Eclogue, which on the day was spoken by the Princesses Helena and Alice, hand in hand:

> Yes, dearest Parents, honour'd, loved and blest,
> Your smile is still the prize we count the best;
> Through long long years together still may Ye,
> In making others happy happiest be.

The Queen commanded Tupper be sent six coloured engravings of the Royal children by Frederic Winterhalter. Just as the poet's sentimental and naive side had entranced the President of the United States, so it pleased Windsor. He was as much of an author as the Queen desired: flattering, easy to understand and with that additional and necessary sense of admonition she had learned from the Prince Consort.

The Queen, like Tupper himself, was a middle-brow. She exacted unquestioning obedience from her entourage and though she sometimes surprised them by her bourgeois dowdiness, they could have seen, if they had chosen to look further afield than the aristocratic society from which they nearly all sprang, their style of Court life already replicated in tens of thousands of homes. The Queen was, as she had to be, the most Victorian of all Victorians. Tupper understood this with more ease than many of his contemporaries. Her habits of thrift, her sometimes errant taste in clothes and furniture, her little vanities were all as familiar to him as his own social habits.

Only a few days after the masque of the seasons, the Queen remarked that Vicky, her eldest child, was already assuming a woman's form. In the following year, when she was 15 years old, the Princess Royal was introduced at Balmoral to Crown Prince Frederick of Prussia. The Prince was handsome but as Lord Granville and others privately considered, a little slow on the uptake. Albert tried but failed to teach him *vingt-et-un*, the simplest of all card games. His general conversation with the royal family was a mixture of correctness and very understandable terror. However, one day, on a pony trail in the hills above Balmoral, he jumped down and plucked a sprig of white heather which he presented to the plump and ruddy-faced Vicky. It was found among her papers when she died.

The engagement lasted three years, during which time the Queen bore her ninth and last child. In 1857 the Princess and her Prussian fiancé were seen together in public for the first time at the Manchester Art Exhibition. Tupper was on hand with two sonnets – one to the Princess, one to Frederick – and was delighted to hear through an intermediary that the Queen wanted a lyric from him when the wedding finally took place.

Meanwhile, the Levee at Windsor that June was the largest ever commanded by the Queen. Tupper had the recently published 30th edition of *Proverbial Philosophy* rebound in white Morocco and cream-coloured satin for the Princess and Prussian blue for Frederick. He begged leave to present them as gifts to the young couple. At the Levee, he overheard the Queen murmur his name to Prince Frederick and Archduke Maximilian of Austria. Before he left he was delighted and astonished to be asked back the next day to present his gifts with his own hand.

This honour was interrupted by a slight hiccup. When he turned up at the appointed hour he was met by an apologetic Colonel Phipps of the Privy Purse who explained that the foreign Princes had misunderstood the arrangements and gone off to Osborne on the Isle of Wight. However, the Queen now desired him to present himself on Sunday, after church. Tupper cautiously enquired as to the correct etiquette for, as far as he knew, the Royal Family had never entertained a private individual in this way since George III had summoned Dr Johnson. Mr Batchelor, the Chief Page, was consulted and indeed never before in his 45 years of service could he remember such a thing. 'So I had the course clear to act according to the light of Nature,' Tupper commented blithely.

On Sunday he arrived at Windsor half an hour early for a one o'clock appointment and was taken by the eldery and doddery Mr Batchelor to the Picture Gallery, where the presentation was to take place. After an agonising wait, there was 'a suppressed hum of voices and a pattering of steps in an adjoining room... and in a minute appeared the advanced guard of gentlemen ushers and lords in waiting; then a man in black walking backwards, – and then the Queen with all her following and family.'

Tupper had been told to stand still and wait to be addressed. The Queen called him forward and said 'in a clear kind voice with a smile, "I thank you, Mr Tupper for your beautiful poetry: and my children are here to thank you too." Then she added, "And my daughter is here to receive your book." '

Proverbial Philosophy, which had redeemed the dullness of old Nat Peckham in the New York backwoods, had been the consolation of a Dartmoor convict and lightened the hours of the Philadelphia insane, was perched on a nearby ottoman, wrapped in crisp white paper and tied with a silk ribbon. For a moment Tupper was uncertain of the protocol.

'Have I your Majesty's permission to give it to the Princess?'

'Most certainly, Mr Tupper. My daughter wishes to take the volume directly from yourself.'

Vicky was given her copy and then Frederick his. Albert presented his son the Prince of Wales, who seemed to want to offer a handshake, but Tupper was in bowing mode and there was a few minutes of mocking and mowing before, as he put it, 'the cavalcade moved on.' Batchelor led him back down the echoing corridors and he was ushered out of the Castle by porters and footmen into the sudden dizzying ordinariness of a Sunday lunchtime.

It was the apogee of his reputation. His friend Gladstone, though he was the Member for Oxford, was for the time being a man without a party and possibly without a future – 'Everyone detests Gladstone,' the political diarist Charles Greville noted cheerfully. Tupper had by comparison been granted a distinction rarely granted to any commoner, poet or not. It was in his nature to sentimentalise the occasion, casting himself as some sort of honoured and reclusive uncle, brought forward to deliver a benediction on the young Royals; and he was of course wrong about that. In the years ahead, it would seem to increasing numbers of people that he was wrong about most things. For the moment, his head was in the clouds. He went into Windsor and drew a sketch map of who stood where when the presentations had been made.

The Prince Consort died in 1861. *Punch*'s loyal and generous assertion that the country 'had shared her joy and will not be denied to share her grief' was small consolation to the Queen, nor did the sentiment last very long. Victoria's almost complete withdrawal from public life at first alarmed and then disgusted her subjects. Ministers who visited her on matters of state at Osborne, to which she had fled, considered she was seriously unbalanced: for the first few months there were rumours of an impending abdication. Just at the time the country at large had found a new stride, a new sense of confidence, the Queen had gone to live on an island of grief and desolation. For some years to come she slept with Albert's nightgown in her arms.

It was well-known that while Albert was alive, the Royal Household was sober-sided and earnest to a fault. The Queen was at one stage forced to insist that she spoke quite as much English to her husband as she did German: the impression remained of a family devoted to tastes and habits that were not entirely British in character. Whenever John Bull was led out by the satirists or ballad-mongers to deliver a clout to affectation or stupidity, his old-fashioned, country-squire simplicity, his good-natured common sense was always bracing. Though the radical tone of *Punch* had softened gently under the editorship of Mark Lemmon, a man who shared many of John Bull's most amiable qualities, the British taste for sardonic and irreverent commentary went undiminished.

Tupper fell victim to it. His fame was more or less synchronous with the first 20 years of the Queen's reign. He was the last to realise that those innocent days were, by the death of Albert, extinguished. In 1858 the *National Review* published in its July issue a scathing article headed 'Charlatan Poetry: Martin Farquhar Tupper'. It wounded him terribly. This was not just a case of grubbing satirists turning against him. Here was a revolt of the opinion-makers. The *Athenaeum* had never liked him, the fledgling

Saturday Review was a ruthless and relentless critic. Tupper's constant excursions into daily journalism, either with indignant political commentary or megaphone-strength moral uplift, were never well-judged and now began to attract more derision than praise. It dawned on him gradually that he was yesterday's man.

Proverbial Philosophy itself was part of the problem. For all his unquenchable energies, Tupper was a one-book author. He did not have it in him to sit still and think, nor could his mind stretch to new ideas, drawn from new circumstances. The smothered parson in him had always stopped him from asking too many uncomfortable questions and residence in the country as a sort of supernumerary squire further blunted his edge. It could be said that Tennyson also lived apart from London, but then Tennyson was a genius. When Tupper looked out of his study window, he saw only the lawn and the garden roller. It was more comforting to glance away and let his eye range over the many editions of his one great book. What wonderful things he had to say, he was convinced he had already said.

There remained Gladstone. Ever since leaving Christ Church, he felt himself able to praise and scold Gladstone the parliamentarian as from the lofty vantage of a respected author who was also the conscience of the country. In 1855 he had written to him on the subject of pursuing the Russians beyond the fall of Sebastopol and the end of the Crimean war.

As I take quite an opposite view of patriotism from you as respects England v. Russia (though I give you credit for equal if not greater conscientiousness) I cannot conceal from myself that my honesty would be in a dilemma, if, under present circumstances, called upon publically to stand on your side. I could not duteously do it, – however tempted by an attachment deeply rooted and I believe immortal; but I could not duteously and there's an end of it.

This is still the language of undergraduate squabbles aired on heated rambles through the Oxford fields. Tupper was very startled to get by return of post a stinging letter from a Gladstone he hardly knew – the mature politician who could barely contain his irritation. Tupper's main argument was that

Gladstone's endorsement of Russia meant in some way a religious move towards Rome. Was his friend tempted in this awful direction? Gladstone hammered his old Christ Church friend into the ground like a tentpeg, giving him a history lesson into the bargain. It included this phosphorescent sentence: 'If you will ask the Pope personally, or get someone else to ask him, his opinion as to my proceedings as to Rome, it may throw some light upon this matter.'

Tupper was chastened. From that moment, the basis of the friendship changed and grew more one-sided. He began to send Gladstone little unwanted gifts, things taken from his own study, such as a statue of Horus or an ancient coin. These and his incurable habit of offering advice and admonishment were acknowledged with polite but non-committal replies. We know that in his lifetime Gladstone received letters from over 12,000 correspondents – Tupper seems to have had no real sense of this. He was presuming on an intimacy that had not outlasted the Oxford years.

One of the more unfortunate thoughts that occurred to him from time to time was that his old friend should attempt to be more popular. It was a sign of Tupper's essential naivety and want of real perspective. In 1862 Gladstone, as Chancellor of the Exchequer, visited Tyneside. On 7 October he spoke in Newcastle at a clamorous dinner for 500 people and the next day went down the Tyne at the head of a flotilla of boats. For more than twenty miles the banks were crowded with miners who had come out of the pits to greet him. Every so often there was a salute of guns – fowling pieces and decorative cannon dragged from the lawns of local squires. His biographer said it was like 'the reception of a king'. This was the difference between politics and literature: some at least of those who greeted Gladstone so effusively were also readers of *Proverbial Philosophy* and its anodyne preachments. That was all well and good, but what this stiff and awkward figure in the scruffy little Tyneside steamer could give them was the vote.

From the 1860s, Tupper's name became synonymous

with poor poetry and the sort of sentiments that attracted shop-girls and servants. The comic press fastened its fangs upon him. Tyro humorists, very often unlicked cubs on provincial newspapers, tossed his name to and fro like a pack of vicious dogs. He became a national figure of fun, not much helped by his unfortunate habit of continuing to publish everything he wrote, the bad along with the good. The attacks on him were completely shameless – and the game was all the funnier because he so completely failed to give in:

Go on, Detraction! Take a mile of rope,
You'll hitch the noose ere long, I more than hope.

Some of the spite shown to him can be traced to what is now a very familiar habit of mind among the English: newspaper envy of the rich and successful. Tupper was one of its first victims. Once the mob would have gone round and broken his windows. Now they had better, crueller weapons at their disposal. This, for example, from a spoof advertisement for patent medicines; 'No. 101,486. M. F.

Tupper, Esq., poet, of confirmed vacuity of mind, wandering thoughts, and general softness of the brain. An almost hopeless case.' Or this, from Professor *Punch*'s Dreambook: 'To dream that you have written all Mr Tupper's Works (and on waking to find that you haven't) is very lucky.' In the papers left at his death is a letter from a hack apologising for attacking him without even knowing him or reading his major works. A few weeks later the same man libelled him again. The public, that new phenonenon, had made him and could as easily unmake him.

There was a widespread belief that he was very rich and could stand a little cutting down to size. This was far from the truth. Just as if to point up the difference between the real world and its imagined and proverbial wholeness, Tupper lost the remainder of his savings in a bank crash; other investments he made were equally disastrous. While his daughters continued as models of obedience and propriety, there was grievous financial misery with his wayward eldest son, Martin Charles Selwyn Tupper. The boy had turned into a dissolute and drunken disgrace.

Tupper and his family outside Albury House in 1864

When he was 22, his father purchased him a commission into the 29th Foot (Worcestershire Regiment). He went straight in as a Captain at a cost of about £1,800, the sort of flourish Tupper could afford in the days of his pomp. The gallant young soldier drank and gambled his father's money away until in 1866 Tupper had seen enough. Presented with a bill for £1000, he refused to pay and Captain Tupper was cashiered.

On the whole he has cost me some £5,000, and all to gain ruined health and damaged character! Poor dear fellow, – so noble and gentlemanly and popular and beloved – and all this human treasure to go to the dogs, like offal.

His son had not finished with him yet. The following year Tupper rushed to a cheap hotel in Jermyn Street where he found Martin in the throes of delirium tremens. He sent him to an asylum in St John's Wood to recover and once he had, the wastrel immediately ran off with the 'bad woman' who had helped him drink himself crazy. At God knows what cost to his belief in the goodness of other people, Tupper recovered his son a second time and sent him to Brazil on remittance. The Southern Hemisphere could not hold him either and he died of the cholera in London ten years later. He was buried in Albury churchyard, where one day his father and mother would join him.

The bad investments, the cost of raising his children and the ruinous efforts to help his eldest son all conspired to drive Tupper down into that numerous class, the genteel poor. He let Albury House and lived a nomadic sort of life along the South Coast, flitting from one rented house to another, trying to keep up the fiction of a literary gentleman of means. For a brief moment or two, he had some hope of becoming the Queen's Librarian, trusting to Victoria's previous good opinion of him. There too his fame had grown dusty. Victoria found his application quite unsuitable, even risible, and he had the honour of having his name decorated in her journal by examples of her famously fractious underlinings and exclamation marks.

A little later, when Gladstone cautiously suggested he might be added to the Bounty List and given some kind of pension, the Queen again refused. She had found a more worthy candidate for that in James Hain Friswell, whose own Tupperish work was *A Gentle Life* which ran into 20 or more editions, one of which the Queen commanded should be dedicated to herself.

Tupper was approaching 60. In 1870 he was thrown from a carriage at Albury and had his right hand crushed. (A son, William, had been killed in an almost identical accident in South Africa). Wearied by pain and using his daughter Mary to write down his words, he extemporised:

Oh trials and troubles and losses in life !
What are ye but simples to strengthen my soul?
And the care and the riot, the wear and the strife,
But spurrings and whippings to speed to the Goal?
Yea, – trampled affections, yea – hopes that are crushed,
Ambition laid low, – the best mercy to pride, –
Are comforted all and their murmurings hushed
By Jireh-Jehovah, the Lord will provide.

He was actually in the middle of dictating a bread-and-butter letter to Gladstone when he composed this: it is a pointer to his essentially facile gift. A fondness for words and a few tried and tested lyrical tricks always came naturally to him. The purpose of the letter Mary was writing out was to thank Gladstone for an ex-gratia government payment of £400, which Tupper suspected was drawn from some slush fund for the secret service. This clumsy and impulsively added stanza was just the sort of thing that had brought him low – it added nothing to his reputation as a poet and its piety was, even to someone of Gladstone's tastes, commonplace.

By 1870, Dickens was dead, as was Thackeray. Tupper-bating had gone on for so long that even some of his worst enemies in the press had begun to say enough was enough. His hair and beard were white now and his over-hearty and old-fashioned manner was treated more indulgently as a relic of the past, that self-deceiving and unregenerate past that the Victorian middle class had begun to learn how to reprehend. Life was quite as serious as Tupper always said it was, but it was to be made better by lawyers and accountants, engineers and family doctors, not poets. Samuel Smiles and his *Self-Help* (1859) was of far greater use to the aspiring artisan or the clerk who sat at his desk for £2 a week and wondered what existence was all about. Grit, determination and hard work was Smiles's answer. A call for better state education, more public libraries, a grasp of what made machines efficient and banks prosper, an extension of the vote and a corresponding assumption of civic duties by the newly enfranchised – all these were advocated by Smiles and made him a representative man of his age. More than 100,000 copies of *Self-Help* were in circulation by 1880 and the book was translated into a dozen or more languages. Proverbial wisdom, no matter how elevated in tone, could not compete.

VI

In his old age Tupper turned to invention – always a little too late at the Patent Office, always blissfully ignorant of practicalities. His rubber horseshoe, designed for frosty weather, was found to disintegrate within a day. It was no more a winner than his paddle steamer 'for war or commerce', the wheels to be placed in the middle of the ship, 'coming out where the keel usually is'. His scheme for a tunnel from Southampton to the Isle of Wight met with no takers, nor was the Astronomer Royal much enthused by the Tupper method of making an artificial eclipse of the sun. It was to be done by erecting a vast metal disc between it and observers. The warship's hull that bristled like a porcupine in order to repel boarders was indignantly rejected by the Admiralty. Nobody bought his plan for essence of tea and his prototype fountain pen either clogged up or dribbled.

A shrewd mind and a generous one might have

concluded that what inspired these 'addled eggs' was not scientific curiosity but pride of life. Tupper simply would not be silenced. 'It isn't the tenant that grows old, but the house,' the composer Gounod once lamented when he realised he was perceived by others as ancient history. Just as Gounod was always the nervy and libidinous Prix de Rome student torn between the flesh and the spirit, so Tupper was always the owlish schoolboy leaning on the sundial at Albury. What came out of him, the inventions no less than the poetry, was the passionate innocence of the child, drawn from a well that never dried. Tupper was one of those happy people for whom every idea is a good one.

One afternoon in 1882, at a demonstration of Hindoo juggling at the Crystal Palace, some mothers were beguiled when a very pleasant old gentleman shared his chocolate drops with their children. The grown-ups felt sure this was a man of importance. Pausing at the gift stall on the way out, they saw that their neighbour was none other than Martin Tupper, famous enough to be a postcard beaming down at them from the racks. 'I have preserved the chocolate drops as relics,' one of the women wrote. 'The children may appreciate him when they grow up.' She was not yet 30 and Tupper was 72. The gap between them was more than generational. What he was before she was born – when the Crystal Place was not in Sydenham but Hyde Park (with 'A Hymn to all Nations' as one of its exhibits) – had vanished as dramatically as crinolines and stovepipe hats. He was from another era altogether, a wavery old man with a Father Christmas beard and very small feet and hands.

Given the loyalty of his American audience, it was almost inevitable that he would be drawn back across the Atlantic one last time, a trip he undertook in 1876. The idea was to make a reading tour to raise money for his family. The centrepiece of his visit was an unpaid engagement to speak at the Brooklyn Tabernacle, where the youthful and dynamic Thomas De Witt Talmage preached to congregations (a better word might be audiences) of more than five thousand. If you liked your church low – and by now Tupper did – then the Tabernacle was the only show in town. Talmage was the prototype of all celebrity preachers. Three times married, he lived in great luxury and ran his church as a branch of show business. If a thing was worth doing – even or perhaps especially a religious thing – it was worth doing well. When Tupper got off his Cunard ship *Abyssinia*, there waiting on the dock was Talmage's coach-and-four, attended by a black driver in livery. He was whisked off at once to Brooklyn.

The New York press were not quite so enthusiastic about their distinguished visitor this time around. He was still a curiosity but a rather fusty one. The *New York Herald* gave him a notice on the editorial page, the dryness of which would have stopped many another heart. After conceding that he had not written as well as Tennyson, Wordsworth, Keats and Coleridge, he had at least written more. 'Quantity has its merit, as well as quality,' the article concluded slyly, inviting readers to share a joke which once in America would have been no joke at all. Some enterprising journalist asked him whether he objected to this kind of attention. Tupper employed a favourite simile. 'I don't care, I want them to. You see, battledore and shuttlecock. You beat the shuttlecock hither and thither, back and forth, round and round, and that keeps it up.'

And to oblige the journalist he jumped up from his chair and, his gold glasses bouncing off his chest, leaped about the room, beating with his fists to indicate how fame worked. It made wonderful copy. The grave and earnest moralist had given way to a man who merely wanted to stay in the game. Tupper had not finished:

> I live quietly at my home near London, but the newspapers will be after me with a great deal of good-natured badinage... They put me in the funny papers sometimes and my children will come running and say, 'Papa, you're in *Punch*, you're in *Fun*'; but I say, laughing, 'Well, I don't care.'

The kindest of his American critics took this confession for what it was, the rattle of an essentially simple man. Now that Tupper had actually grown to look like the sage that stumbles from his green grotto in the woods in order to buttonhole the unwary traveller, paradoxically the magic had fled. The philosopher in him had become the cheery old bore that sidles up to you on the bridge to explain that you are fishing on the wrong stretch of the river.

Talmage, however, had a very secure handle on his guest. On 22 October Tupper accompanied the divine on stage before some 6,000 of the devout, assembled for Sunday morning service. The famous Tabernacle choir, which of course still exists and records today, swept into 'Coronation'. Reporters from the *New York Herald*, the *World* and the *Sun* were on hand at the back of the hall to give Tupper a gentle drubbing. Talmage may have sensed this. 'None of us,' he boomed out 'will mistake this for a lecturing occasion, for the poem we are to hear is a sermon in blank verse. Many world poems have been inspired by the wine cup: this one was inspired by God, and consolation is the burden of the poem.'

At which he sat down with a suitably thoughtful frown. The man from the *World* was specially delighted to see what he considered Tupper's affectation of solemn prayer before commencing. There was the usual stage business with squeaky chairs and a lectern that was too high for the poet; but then the plump little Englishman began an hour's reading with this, from the second series of *Proverbial Philosophy*:

Gird up thy mind to contemplation, trembling inhabitant of earth:

Tenant of a hovel for a day, thou art heir of the Universe forever!

For, neither congealing of the grave, nor gulphing waters of the firmament,

Nor expansive airs of heaven, nor dissipative fires of Gehenna,

Nor rust of rest, nor wear, nor waste, nor loss, nor chance nor change,

Shall avail to quench or overwhelm the spark of soul within thee.

That, the *World* reporter was forced to admit an hour later, was telling them. The papers still had their fun with him. It was noted how he paused for dramatic effect from time to time to gaze up at the chandelier as if contemplating all eternity. At other times he 'peered like a blind duck'. To many, Talmage, a famously goodlooking man, seemed uneasy. Nevertheless it is in the Brooklyn Tabernacle performance that we can look for the hero in Tupper. He gave other readings in America in that year and he had previously toured Southern England with recitals, but this moment defines him. Talmage was in Brooklyn to fight sin and fan the immortal spark but he was also tough on civic corruption and public incompetence. His own sermons were racy denunciations of the ugly city his congregation knew only too well lay right outside the Tabernacle walls. Tupper knew as much about Brooklyn as he did about Bermondsey, which was to say nothing at all. What he did know about, in his cranky oddball way, was the human yearning for something better than what is. When Tupper read that day, it was the journalists that were made to look ridiculous.

Tupper was all the same a vain man and, much more damagingly, an incautious one. Even a bit of common sense or a few moments of reflection in his youth, when the next bad poem was about to be posted into the letterbox mouth, would have saved him from much of the derision later heaped on his head. He knew how to bring himself before a public but when he got there, he did not always make best use of his opportunity. Nevertheless, very few people who ever met Martin Tupper made him their enemy and he in turn bore not the slightest malice towards another human being. Thirty years after the Tabernacle reading, one of the journalists who had been present remembered the poet calling to see him.

It was not a pleasant moment for me when his card was sent in but Mr Tupper proved to be one of the most amiable and kind-hearted of gentlemen. He laughed over what I had written of him, and showed such an utter absence of resentment that I grew heartily ashamed... When I learned how thoroughly its author was entitled to respect, the book no longer seemed to be amusing.

His second American tour was extensive but unrewarding. Back in England, he and his wife settled at 13 Cintra Park in Upper Norwood, South London. Though he still owned Albury House, which he had let out to rent, Cintra Park, with its ugly interiors yet generous views over the Crystal Palace grounds, finally kennelled all his ambition. The house was an end-of-terrace on three floors and was partly – as happens to old people – a museum to their dreams. Every edition of his works was ranged round the walls of one room and here too was his collection of coins, his agates, his designs for inventions and the curiously juvenile drawings he made of lofty religious subjects. His desk was always cluttered with correspondence. Recently, he had begun the pleasant habit of writing encouraging notes to new authors: very few refused the invitation to reply. His was so much a voice from the past that many people thought him already dead.

If somewhere in the neighbourhood was the young woman who had preserved his chocolate drops for their curiosity value, the house in Cintra Park was a treasure trove of far greater dimensions. Tupper hardly ever threw away a piece of paper that might cast light on himself – the tribulations as well as the triumphs. Much of his correspondence went back half a century. If there was foolishness in his self-love it was utterly harmless, in the particular sense that he could no longer harm himself.

Or almost not. When the poet laureate Tennyson was made a Baron at the end of 1883, Tupper wrote to the *Times* hoping wistfully this would lead the way to further honours being accorded to literary men. It was his last despairing throw of the dice. The badly judged letter irritated Gladstone, who had broached the subject of a barony to Tennyson in the romantic circumstances of a luxury liner's maiden voyage round Britain. Gladstone admired Tennyson greatly and when he got a letter from the fastnesses of Upper Norwood angling for at least a knighthhood, his reply was icy:

You are aware that authorship even when attended with great distinction is not commonly marked by the grant of honours. The case of Mr Tennyson has appeared to be capable, taking all its features together, of being treated by way of exception. But I think to make other exceptions, especially at this time, would tend to break down the rule, and it would involve me in difficulties of selection such as I could not face.

Tupper was never to receive the final public honour he so much desired. Nevertheless, when he sat in his study and examined the groaning shelves of Tupperiana in all its editions and languages and swept an eye over his cluttered desk, he could count himself a success. One way or another, as his bulging scrapbooks testified, his name had been on everyone's lips for over four decades. Simply to say to a stranger 'I am Tupper' was to guarantee a response of some kind – if he was not a knight of the realm he was at least a national institution. His chocolate drops were worth saving.

Issy and he had somehow come through. Very plump now, and exceedingly quiet in her habits, Issy's pleasures were in her daughters, perhaps particularly the first-born, Ellin, whose common sense and even temper had helped the family through some difficult times. Mary, like her sister, Ellin, was a poet, and Margaret, the ever faithful Peggie, a painter and poet. The surviving son, Walter, was unmarried and saw out his life as a minor Post Office official. Looked at from Issy's chair in the house, these Tuppers were modest and respectable people like all the other families in Cintra Park. In her eyes, they were none the

Tupper in his 76th year

worse for that. Tupper's hunger for fame was never an appetite shared by his wife and children. They had enjoyed good times and bad and had on occasions lived extremely comfortably. It mattered much less to them that their father had hobnobbed with Royalty: it may have mattered more that some of the public obloquy that visited him fell on their own heads. Now, when the rocket had almost burned out, 'dearest little Par', as his daughter Peggie invariably addressed him, was to his neighbours and to the gate-keepers at the Crystal Palace, where he held a season ticket, the same cheery fellow he had always been. If he was a little odd, then by how much was he any odder than some of the other residents of Cintra Park, a road which boasted two ministers of religion, the unmarried lady proprietors of a school for girls, Colonel Phelps and his dentist son and – at the end of the street – a Salvation Army hostel?

On 26 November, the Tuppers celebrated their golden wedding. Four weeks later, Issy dropped dead under the Christmas decorations. Tupper was told by the doctors that had she lived she would have been paralysed. 'God doeth all things well,' he responded calmly. In his study was the half-completed manuscript of his autobiography, called *My Life as an Author*. He grieved for his wife but he laboured to bring out his last book. Like all the rest of his work, it was patchily written. The tone was painfully jocular, as if in the end this supremely self-assertive man had reached out beyond himself to discover the emptiness that surrounded him. It was battledore and shuttlecock with no one to keep the game alive at the other end of the room. Though the reviews were kindly, there was no second edition.

A year after Issy's death, his daughter Ellin was reading to him in the cramped light of a November morning when she glanced up to see that he was unconscious. For three days he hovered between life and death, the victim of a stroke. The Queen sent him a message and the newspapers reported his condition sympathetically. Then, little by little, he regained his faculties, enough to speak and remember who he was and the names of his children.

He had planned great things for the Jubilee Year of 1887 when the national outpouring of affection took the Queen so much by surprise. Tupper had predicted this and had spent the previous summer writing an historical preface to some solemn doggerel on the subject. He considered Victoria's reign unique in the history of the world and in this he was not alone: the whole country went on an emotional binge in 1887 and lucky were those who could remember the Coronation, as could Tupper.

He lingered another three years, able to walk – indeed to be taken to hear the bands play at the Crystal Palace on fine summer afternoons – but never again to read or write. His desk was emptied and polished and the study full of his own books was lovingly dusted every day. But he was done with all that. The trickle of letters that came in now were read to him by his daughters and his replies were haphazardly dictated. Right to the very end, Ellin continued to paste any notice of him, any slight reference, into the last of the 25 albums that chronicled his life. He died on 29 November 1889 and one of the first things his son Walter did, even while the blinds were being pulled down and a notice posted on the front door to inform the anxious neighbours, was to write to Gladstone.

Tupper was not a man of letters in the ordinary sense of the phrase. As the *Times* obituary gently pointed out, 'his strange and unique position in literature [was] a tribute to the British heart rather than to its intellect.' The author of *Proverbial Philosophy* did not impose himself upon his public: he was made by them, and when they had enough of him, he was unmade. Without the stammer, he would undoubtedly have entered the church and made his contribution there. He had a famously rich and crotchety neighbour in Norwood who could have shown the way. The great Baptist preacher Charles Haddon Spurgeon, who so thrilled and entranced huge congregations in the mid-Victorian period, is a pointer to what Tupper might have become had he too taken the cloth.

It seemed that George III had patted him on the head in vain, for Martin Tupper had set off on a path that was wide enough to begin with, but dwindled inexorably until he was quite alone in the forest. All the same, three monarchs later, Victoria remembered him well enough to command her secretary Sir Henry Ponsonby to send a telegram to Cintra Park: 'The

Queen is much grieved to hear of your father's death and desires to express her sincere sympathy.' The dazed family took out the glue-pot for the last time and added to the scrapbook this one last record.

Tupper survived all his brothers, his wife and three of his children before finally falling silent. He was buried at Albury in bitter cold in the same grave as Issy and next to his reckless and wayward son. There were no mourners from the literary world and no memorial services were held in London. A new joint headstone was ordered and under Tupper's name and dates was the legend 'He being dead yet speaketh'. Under Issy's name and dates was written 'In death they were not divided.'

Like the Ogibwa Indians who had provided a translation to his 'Hymn for All Nations', the print of Tupper's foot was erased from the earth and his name sank as surely as a stone flung into the icy waters of Tupper Lake. Fifty six years after that final telegram of condolence from Queen Victoria, all of Tupper's treasured scrapbooks were found heaped up in a Bloomsbury bookseller's, having survived the Blitz, but not the judgment of a crueller age.

OTHER SHORT BOOKS:

General non-fiction

British Teeth
An excruciating journey from the dentist's chair
to the rotten heart of a nation
William Leith

The Strange World of Thomas Harris
Inside the mind of the creator of Hannibal Lecter
David Sexton

Funeral Wars
How lawyer Willie Gary turned a petty dispute about
coffins into a multimillion-dollar morality play
Jonathan Harr

Last Drink to LA
Cleaning up on the West Coast of America:
confessions of an AA survivor
John Sutherland

Your Pedigree Chum
A tale of dogged determination, from ancient
bones to canine clones
James Langton

Nurse Wolf & Dr Sacks
This is New York... A dominatrix
and a doctor share tales of the city
Paul Theroux

Biography/Memoirs

The Voice of Victorian Sex: A.H. Clough
Rupert Christiansen

A Material Girl: Bess of Hardwick
Kate Hubbard

Inventor of the Disposable Culture: King Camp Gillette
Tim Dowling

Last Action Hero of the British Empire: Cdr John Kerans
Nigel Farndale

**The Hungarian Who Walked to Heaven:
Alexander Csoma de Koros**
Edward Fox

The Hated Wife: Carrie Kipling
Adam Nicolson

**The Real Tadzio: Thomas Mann's 'Death in Venice'
and the boy who inspired it**
Gilbert Adair

In Love and War: A Letter to my Parents
Maria Corelli

UK retail price: £4.99/Sales and distribution:
Faber & Faber